Original title:
Broad Anthems Beneath the Crystal Bend

Author: Swan Charm
ISBN HARDBACK: 978-1-80559-178-8
ISBN PAPERBACK: 978-1-80559-677-6

Harmonic Blessings of the Evening Tide

The sun dips low, a fiery glow,
Whispers of night begin to flow.
Gentle waves embrace the shore,
A calming balm, forevermore.

Stars awaken in the sky,
As twilight breathes a soft goodbye.
Moonlight dances on the sea,
A serenade of harmony.

Vibrant Echoes of Nature's Serenade

In the forest, life awakes,
Birds in chorus, joy it stakes.
Whispers through the rustling leaves,
Nature's song, the heart believes.

Rippled streams that laugh and play,
Meadows bright with blooms display.
Every hue a vibrant call,
Echoes of life, embracing all.

Spheres of Resonance and Reflection

In the stillness, thoughts collide,
Mirrored souls and hearts confide.
Waves of echoes swirl around,
In this sphere, serenity's found.

In reflections, truths arise,
Hidden depths beneath the skies.
Silent whispers intertwine,
As the cosmos starts to shine.

The Spirit of Windsong in Shifting Sands

Across the dunes, the breezes play,
Carrying dreams from far away.
Whispers soft as twilight glows,
In the night, the winds compose.

Footprints vanish in the night,
With the dawn, a new insight.
Windsong hums a timeless tune,
Guiding hearts to brave the dunes.

Illuminating Tunes of the Silent Dawn

In whispers soft, the night withdraws,
The silver moon begins to fade.
Awakening dreams in gentle pause,
The dawn emerges, light cascades.

Birds sing songs of morning's grace,
Each note a thread, a golden ray.
With every breath, we find our place,
In sunlight's warmth, we greet the day.

Shadows dance on fields of dew,
As petals yawn in blush and bloom.
The world revives, a canvas new,
Beneath the sun, dispelling gloom.

Echoes of a night once past,
Fade into hues of pink and blue.
The moments stretch, so sweet, so vast,
Inviting hearts to start anew.

With every dawn, a chance to shine,
A symphony of light and air.
Illuminated, souls align,
In harmony, we find our care.

Fables of the Winds We Carry

The winds tell tales of olden dreams,
In rustling leaves, the stories flow.
Each breeze a laugh, a sigh, it seems,
Whispers of paths that we may know.

Through valleys deep, where shadows play,
And mountains tall that touch the skies,
The winds embrace both night and day,
In echoes sweet, their wisdom lies.

With every gust, a memory stirs,
Of wanderers, lost yet found.
The heart of nature softly purrs,
As lullabies in silence sound.

In twilight's glow, the currents weave,
A tapestry of time and space.
So listen close, and you will believe,
The winds will guide you with their grace.

Together we dance, both wild and free,
As stories spin upon the breeze.
In every breath, we find the key,
To realms beyond, where spirits tease.

Nature's Whispers Beneath the Stars

In quiet nights, the cosmos gleams,
And nature hums a lullaby.
The stars align, fulfill our dreams,
As whispered secrets drift on high.

Moonbeams kiss the silent streams,
Where crickets play their soft refrain.
A symphony of night redeems,
The weary hearts that seek refrain.

The ancient trees, in shadows cast,
Hold stories wrapped in leaves of lore.
With every sigh, the night holds fast,
And beckons us to seek for more.

Upon the breeze, the scented trails,
Carry hints of earth's embrace.
In nature's arms, the heart prevails,
Each moment cherished, time and space.

Beneath these stars, we come alive,
As whispers weave through darkened skies.
With open hearts, we learn to thrive,
In union with the universe's cries.

Arias of the Crystal Cascades

Where waters sing and mountains rise,
The crystal cascades flow with grace.
In every splash, the world complies,
With melodies that time can't erase.

The chorus swells, a vibrant tune,
As droplets dance on stones so bare.
Beneath the sun or silver moon,
The arias fill the fragrant air.

Each brooklet flows with tales untold,
Of journeys made through vale and glen.
In harmony, the stories unfold,
In nature's voice, we find our zen.

The whispers of the water's hymn,
Awaken souls with every note.
In rushing streams, life's lights don't dim,
As crystal melodies softly float.

So come and listen, let it be,
The rhythm guides, the heart it sways.
In every drop, a memory,
The arias of the cascades plays.

Luminescent Harmonies in the Wild

In the forest, whispers glow,
Gentle breezes dance and flow.
Leaves shimmer with a soft delight,
Nature sings in the calm of night.

Moonlight casts its silver grace,
Creatures pause, all find their place.
Stars twinkle in a velvet sky,
Echoes linger, time drifts by.

The river hums a soothing song,
Where shadows play, we all belong.
Branches sway in rhythmic tune,
The night awakens under the moon.

Crickets chirp their nightly cheer,
Notes of joy for all to hear.
A serenade of life anew,
In this wild, a spark to pursue.

Together in this vibrant scene,
Harmony flows, serene and keen.
With each note, the world expands,
In luminescent, gentle hands.

A Tapestry of Celestial Notes

Across the heavens, music weaves,
Threads of starlight in gentle eves.
Constellations hum a tune,
Galaxies dance beneath the moon.

Whispers of the cosmos rise,
Interstellar lullabies.
Planets turn in perfect dance,
In this vast celestial expanse.

Comets trail with silver strands,
Painting arcs across the lands.
Harmony stitched in cosmic flight,
Awakens dreams in the still of night.

Echoes in the darkened air,
Promises held everywhere.
A chorus formed from dust and fire,
Unleashing songs that never tire.

In this tapestry of delight,
A symphony that feels so right.
Take a breath, let your spirit soar,
In celestial notes, forevermore.

The Symphony of Forgotten Shores

Waves crash softly on the sand,
A melody from a distant land.
Seagulls call with a haunting cry,
Where the ocean meets the sky.

Driftwood lies in silent grace,
Whispers of time in this sacred place.
The tides, they ebb and flow their tune,
Singing secrets beneath the moon.

Shells echo stories of days gone by,
Carried forth with a gentle sigh.
The breeze, it whispers, soft and low,
A symphony that ebbs and flows.

Footprints linger on the shore,
Tales of love and longing, more.
The ocean's heart keeps beating strong,
In forgotten shores, we belong.

Underneath the starlit night,
The sea reflects a glowing light.
In every wave and every chord,
A timeless song that's never bored.

Serenades of the Endless Expanse

In vast skies where the silence hums,
Echoes dance, the spirit comes.
Clouds drift softly in fields of blue,
A serenade, so pure and true.

Mountains stand with a noble grace,
Guarding secrets in their embrace.
Rivers rush with a joyful heartbeat,
Nature's rhythms, ours to meet.

The wind carries tales from afar,
Whistling tunes from each star.
A symphony woven with light and shade,
In endless expanse, memories made.

Fields of gold sway in the breeze,
Nature's chorus brings us ease.
Each moment a note, fleeting yet grand,
A serenade sung for all the land.

Underneath the endless sky,
Let our worries drift and fly.
In the harmony of life's vast song,
We find where our hearts belong.

Chasing Reflections in Liquid Sky

In the calm of twilight's grace,
Ripples dance in soft embrace.
Colors blend, a mirror's play,
Whispers of the end of day.

Clouds drift slowly overhead,
Memories of words unsaid.
Glimmers trace where dreams align,
Within the depths, our hopes entwine.

Stars awaken, one by one,
Kissing dreams that just begun.
Each reflection shows a path,
Pain and joy, the aftermath.

Upon the liquid canvas bright,
We chase illusions of pure light.
Every ripple tells a tale,
In this world where dreams prevail.

So let us chase what lies ahead,
In liquid skies where dreams are fed.
Together in this endless flight,
Chasing reflections toward the night.

Lullabies of Celestial Currents

Underneath the canopy wide,
Cosmic whispers gently glide.
Stars hum softly, lullabies,
Woven light in velvet skies.

Gentle breezes kiss our skin,
Flowing tales of where we've been.
Twilight cradles every dream,
In this flowing, silent stream.

Lunar beams like silver threads,
Wrap around our sleepy heads.
Every note a sweet caress,
In the dark, we find our rest.

Floating through this endless space,
Finding peace in every trace.
Celestial currents guide us near,
Whispering songs for all to hear.

So breathe deeply, let time drift,
Wrapped in love, a cosmic gift.
Lullabies of stars above,
Serenading us with love.

Harmonies of the Gleaming Stream

In the heart of nature's rhyme,
Flowing waters mark the time.
Echoes blend in liquid song,
Where we know we all belong.

Sunlight dances on the waves,
Caressing shores where beauty saves.
Every ripple, every gleam,
Forms a part of nature's dream.

Whispers ride the gentle breeze,
Carrying the scent of trees.
Songs of birds in joyful flight,
Bringing life to day and night.

As we walk this winding path,
Finding peace amidst the wrath.
Harmonies that soothe the soul,
In this stream, we are made whole.

Let the waters guide our hearts,
Where the melody never departs.
Gleaming reflections, serene sights,
Together, we share the heights.

Serenades of the Infinite Flow

In the depth of endless night,
Stars cascade with pure delight.
Flowing softly, time stands still,
Nature's voice, a gentle thrill.

Waves of light in patterns weave,
Telling tales that we believe.
Every current draws us near,
In this rhythm, we have cheer.

Moonlit paths where shadows play,
Guiding dreams that find their way.
Serenades of peace abound,
In the silence, love is found.

Here the rivers sing and flow,
Underneath the starlit glow.
Infinite, the call we hear,
Binding all that we hold dear.

So let us drift on melodies,
Floating freely in the breeze.
With each note, we find our place,
In this flow, we give our grace.

Harmony's Echoes in a Clear Reverie

In the gentle sway of trees,
Echoes dance with every breeze.
Whispers soft, the world aligns,
In the heart, a spark divine.

Melodies rise like morning light,
Colors blend, the day feels bright.
Dreams unfold in whispered song,
As we drift where we belong.

Reveries in twilight glance,
Guiding souls in nature's dance.
Time stands still in tender glow,
Where the softest feelings flow.

Harmony sings through the air,
Filling hearts with gentle care.
In this space, we breathe as one,
Twofold hearts, a life begun.

Melodies of the Shimmering Horizon

Beyond the waves, where dreams abide,
Horizons sing, the worlds collide.
Colors flourish, a vibrant hue,
As the sun bids the night adieu.

Each note carried on the seas,
Stirs the soul; a playful breeze.
Rhythms of the ocean's heart,
Whisper secrets, set apart.

Mirrored skies in twilight's hold,
Tales of love and courage bold.
Brimming bright with flickering light,
In darkness, hope ignites the night.

Shimmering dreams, they rise and fall,
Melodies weave a timeless call.
In the distance, futures gleam,
Woven softly into a dream.

Whispers of the Deep Blue Dream

In depths where shadows gently sway,
Soft whispers guide the lost away.
Underneath the surface gleams,
Lives a world of silent dreams.

Rippling currents, tales untold,
Secrets held in wave's strong fold.
Ocean's heart beats strong and true,
In the night, it sings for you.

Starry skies reflect below,
Waves embrace the moon's soft glow.
In this soundscape, spirits soar,
Listen close, you'll hear the roar.

Each rise and fall, a lullaby,
Dancing beneath the starlit sky.
In the deep, where echoes merge,
Find your peace, let your heart surge.

Songs of the Fractured Light

Fragments sparkle, a crystal dance,
Twinkles caught in time's romance.
Shards of color, stories bind,
Whispers in the light, we find.

Every flicker holds a tale,
In the silence, colors sail.
Nature's brush paints soft divide,
Underneath the sun's wide stride.

In the dusk, reflections wane,
Bridges built where love remains.
In the break of day's embrace,
A symphony of hidden grace.

Songs of light that dance and play,
Guide us through the fleeting day.
With every heartbeat, bright and clear,
Let the fractured light draw near.

Echoed Whispers in the Moonlit Stream

In the hush of night's embrace,
Soft murmurs dance in silver light.
Ripples cradle secrets shared,
Amongst the whispers, hearts take flight.

Underneath the glowing sheen,
Stars confide in the water's grace.
Each echo sings a story old,
Carried upon the night's calm face.

Moonbeams stitch the shadows near,
As dreams collide with flowing streams.
A gentle breeze caresses all,
Binding silence with soft dreams.

In this realm where stillness reigns,
Hope floats on the liquid hue.
The night is woven with such threads,
Where every moment feels brand new.

Time slows down in this pure space,
Where memories drift like fallen leaves.
Each whisper cradled in embrace,
In the stream's song, our spirit weaves.

Verses Beneath the Glimmering Flow

Beneath the canopy of stars,
The river hums a tranquil tune.
Notes of joy and soft despair,
Float in harmony with the moon.

Pebbles glisten in the dark,
Each one tells a tale distinct.
A bond of nature and our hearts,
In shadows where our souls are linked.

The world around us fades away,
When water plays its timeless song.
In every ripple, life unfolds,
Teaches us where we belong.

Along the banks, the whispers grow,
Of hopes and dreams that weave and spin.
Beneath the sky's eternal glow,
A new journey can begin.

In this sweet embrace of night,
We find solace in the stream's breath.
Carried forth on a gentle tide,
Where echoes breathe beyond our death.

Serenades of the Reflective Veil

A curtain drawn in twilight's name,
Reflects the serenades we sing.
The water's surface, a mirror bright,
Where every thought finds its own wing.

Softly brushing against the shore,
The gentle waves hold secrets dear.
In their depths, a world concealed,
A silent song that only we hear.

Beneath the stars, our voices merge,
With echoes of the night's soft breeze.
Each note a shimmering embrace,
Binding our hearts with nature's ease.

In the quietude of this hour,
Our dreams are cradled by the stream.
The night, a stage for whispered vows,
Where love flows deep in every beam.

Held within this tranquil dance,
We find the strength to journey on.
In every ripple, hope reflects,
A canvas painted with the dawn.

Ballads Beneath the Glittering Sky

Underneath the vast expanse,
Ballads rise like mist at dawn.
Every note a tale of life,
In the twilight, gently drawn.

Stars scatter sparks across the dark,
Their twinkling lights a guiding path.
Each whisper carries dreams untold,
In the embrace of nature's wrath.

The breeze sings soft through the trees,
As leaves join in a sweet refrain.
A harmony of fading light,
Where every sorrow meets its gain.

In this realm of silvery hues,
Hope shimmers in the cooling air.
With each verse, a pulse of love,
As hearts entwine in evening's glare.

Through the night, our spirits soar,
In every measure, pure delight.
Together, we shall wander far,
Beneath the glittering sky tonight.

Nature's Choir Among the Pines

Whispers float in the soft breeze,
Leaves dance gently, a tranquil tease.
Birds sing sweet, a melodic tune,
Nature's choir beneath the moon.

Sunlight filters through the green,
Painting shadows, a calming scene.
Branches sway, a soothing grace,
In this quiet, a warm embrace.

Crisp scents rise from the forest floor,
Echoing tales of days of yore.
Rustling ferns with stories spun,
In harmony, all life has begun.

Majestic pine, standing tall,
Guarding secrets, a silent call.
Harmony of whispers and sighs,
In nature's breath, the spirit flies.

As dusk descends, stars alight,
A tapestry of pure delight.
Together, all in silent praise,
Nature's choir, in twilight's haze.

Dreamscapes of the Boundless Ocean

Waves caress the shimmering shore,
Whispers of dreams from ocean's core.
Tides that rise and softly fall,
Echo the secrets, the call of all.

Beneath the surface, life abounds,
Swirling colors, the ocean's sounds.
Coral reefs like painted dreams,
Flow with the rhythm of silver streams.

Sailboats drift under vast, blue skies,
Journeying forth where freedom lies.
Glistening horizons, endless and wide,
Upon the waves, our dreams abide.

Sunsets bleed into the sea,
A canvas bold, pure poetry.
With every hue, hope takes flight,
In the embrace of fading light.

Stars emerge as night takes hold,
Whispering tales from the deep and old.
In dreams we sail through the wide expanse,
By the sea's lullaby, we dance.

Subtle Tones of Echoing Plains

Golden grasses sway in the breeze,
A soft whisper through towering trees.
Rolling hills that stretch so far,
Sketch the horizon, a painted star.

Footsteps echo on dirt paths worn,
Stories linger of battles sworn.
Distant thunder, a warm embrace,
Nature's heartbeat in open space.

Clouds drift slowly, a painter's stroke,
In the silence, the earth awoke.
Sunlight bathes the fields in gold,
Tales of beauty quietly told.

Crows caw loudly, a midday tune,
As shadows dance beneath the moon.
Life abounds in every glance,
In quiet moments, we find our chance.

As dusk descends, colors unfurl,
An evening breeze begins to whirl.
In the vast plains, we find our place,
Subtle tones of nature's grace.

Celestial Cadence Beneath the Moon

Under the glow of a silver sphere,
Night whispers secrets, quiet and clear.
Stars twinkle gently in cosmic dance,
Inviting hearts to take a chance.

Moonlight bathes the world in peace,
A tender balm, a sweet release.
Soft shadows stretch across the land,
Illuminated dreams, perfectly planned.

As crickets sing in rhythmic delight,
Nature's song greets the tranquil night.
The world becomes a canvas bright,
In celestial cadence, hearts take flight.

Dreamers walk under starlit skies,
With wishes whispered, and hopeful sighs.
Each moment holds the universe's glow,
Beneath the moon, our spirits grow.

Closing our eyes to the night's embrace,
In the quietness, we find our place.
In the harmony of moonlit tunes,
We dance along with the dreaming dunes.

Ballads of the Gentle Night Breeze

In whispers soft, the night begins,
The stars alight, like distant sins.
A hush that falls upon the earth,
A tender call of fleeting mirth.

Through rustling leaves, a dance of grace,
The moon reveals her silver face.
Each breath of air, a soothing sigh,
In twilight's arms, we gently lie.

The cool caress, the tranquil sound,
A lullaby that wraps around.
With every note, the heart takes flight,
Embraced by peace, we hold the night.

As shadows blend with dreams anew,
The night reveals its velvet hue.
Together caught in time's embrace,
In gentle night, we find our place.

So let the breeze bring tales untold,
Of whispered hopes and hearts of gold.
With every sigh, the night conspires,
To fan the flames of hidden fires.

Rhapsodies of the Serene Waters

The lake reflects the morning light,
A canvas painted, pure and bright.
Ripples sing a soft refrain,
As dawn awakens, free from pain.

Above, the sky in azure spreads,
While silken waves caress the beds.
In whispered tones, they share their dreams,
With every lilt, the water gleams.

The gentle flow, the timeless dance,
A symphony of sweet expanse.
In every droplet, life resides,
Where nature's magic softly glides.

As twilight beckons, colors blend,
The waters hum, a tranquil friend.
Together we, in silence, sway,
As rhapsodies of peace convey.

With every ripple, secrets flow,
In harmony, the waters know.
And in their depths, a world divine,
A soothing balm, pure and benign.

Songs Carried by the Wandering Cloud

A cloud drifts high, in skies so grey,
It sings of journeys far away.
With every shift, a tale unfolds,
Of whispered dreams and secrets bold.

It dances soft on winds of fate,
A wanderer, it bears no weight.
In gentle sways, it tells of time,
Of mountain peaks, and valleys prime.

Through storms and sun, it paints the air,
In hues of joy, a canvas rare.
The stories shared by breezes light,
Transform the day into the night.

With each soft gust, a melody,
A serenade of wild and free.
It carries hope on silken trails,
As cloud-bound songs ride unseen sails.

So gaze above and heed the call,
For every cloud sings to us all.
With love and loss, the sky connects,
In songs they weave, our hearts reflect.

Fauna's Lullaby in the Meadow

In meadows green, the critters play,
Beneath the sun's warm, golden ray.
With rustling grass and gentle twirls,
They weave a dream where magic swirls.

The fireflies blink, a soft embrace,
As twilight takes the day's bright place.
The crickets chirp a soothing song,
Inviting all to dance along.

Each creature small with hope fulfilled,\nIn nature's arms,
their dreams are stilled.
A lullaby of love takes flight,
In harmony, they greet the night.

The stars emerge, a blanket wide,
While shadows stretch, and fears subside.
In every heartbeat, life resonates,
As moonlight guides through open gates.

So rest, dear ones, in peace tonight,
The meadow sings; it feels so right.
With every sound, a story shared,
In Fauna's lullaby declared.

Serenade at the Water's Edge

Whispers curl upon the breeze,
Moonlight dances on the seas.
Stars above, a twinkling choir,
Hearts entwined, kindled fire.

Waves lap softly at the shore,
Secrets shared forevermore.
In the night, our spirits soar,
A serenade we can't ignore.

Silhouettes beneath the moon,
Nature's night-time, sweet monsoon.
Gentle touch, a lover's song,
In this moment, we belong.

Reflections of our dreams collide,
In the tide, we cast aside.
Melodies wrapped in the night,
Together, everything feels right.

As dawn breaks 'neath the sky's embrace,
All our fears, we shall erase.
Water's edge, where love ignites,
In the serenade, pure delights.

Melodies of the Reaching Sky

High above, the clouds drift slow,
Whispers of the winds that blow.
Golden hues of morning light,
Brush the earth with purest sight.

Birds take flight, a soaring song,
In the vastness, we belong.
Voices rise, as dreams take wing,
In this place, our hearts will sing.

Tales of love and hope unfold,
Through the skies, our hopes we hold.
Every note, a promise made,
In the melodies, we wade.

As the sun begins to gleam,
Life awakens, like a dream.
In our hearts, the rhythm flows,
To the sky, our spirit goes.

Underneath this canvas wide,
Together, we will always glide.
In the heights where eagles soar,
Melodies whisper evermore.

Chords of the Translucent Tides

The ocean hums a timeless tune,
Beneath the watchful, silver moon.
Waves compose a symphony,
In harmony, you and me.

Underneath the surface clear,
Secret worlds draw ever near.
Rippling echoes fill the air,
In this magic, we will share.

Tides that crash, then softly rise,
Hold the truth of whispered lies.
Each chord woven with delight,
Guides our souls through endless night.

As the currents pull us back,
Feel the rhythm, lose the lack.
In this dance, our spirits twine,
Translucent tides, forever shine.

So let the water's song surround,
In this place, our hearts are bound.
Chords that wield an ancient play,
In the tides, we'll drift away.

Rhythms of the Still Waters

In the calm where silence reigns,
Nature whispers soft refrains.
Reflections dance upon the lake,
In this peace, our hearts awake.

Gentle ripples mark the night,
Stars above, a guiding light.
Stillness speaks in tender sighs,
Cradled here, our worries die.

Every heartbeat, synchronized,
With the world that feels so prized.
In the depths, our truths are found,
As still waters echo sound.

Moonbeams cast a silver glow,
On the surface, love will flow.
In this sacred space we meet,
Rhythms pulse, our hearts repeat.

So let the stillness mend our souls,
In the water, we are whole.
Together, in this quiet sphere,
Rhythms hum and draw us near.

Elixirs of the Whispering Woods

In the hush of the green, secrets dwell,
Leaves murmur tales they long to tell.
Mossy paths with soft shadows play,
Elixirs of light chase the dark away.

The breeze dances low, it twirls with grace,
Guiding the way through this enchanted place.
Each step a rhythm, a gentle refrain,
Nature's own song, pure and unchained.

Beneath ancient trees, wisdom is found,
Whispers of magic weave all around.
The heartbeat of earth, steady and true,
Calls to the wanderer, beckoning through.

In twilight's embrace, the shadows take flight,
Elixirs of stars fill the canvas of night.
Twinkling above, the cosmos does gleam,
Inviting the dreamer to drift in a dream.

With every soft breath, the woods softly sigh,
A tapestry woven where wild spirits lie.
Elixirs of love, peace mingled with grace,
In the whispering woods, find your place.

Songs of the Ethereal Sea

Waves crashing gently on silken shore,
Sing of adventures, of treasures galore.
Seagulls cry out, they dance in the breeze,
Songs of the sea bring hearts to their knees.

Beneath the blue depths, mysteries thrive,
Creatures of ocean in harmony strive.
Whispers of coral, shadows of fish,
Each echoing note a tender wish.

The sun dips low, painting skies bright,
A canvas of colors igniting the night.
Songs of the sea, a longing embrace,
Connecting all souls in this vast, sacred space.

The horizon beckons, adventures await,
With every tide change, the world feels great.
Salt on the air, freedom in flow,
Songs of the sea, the heart's gentle glow.

In the stillness, there lies a pearl,
Songs that can change, can shimmer, can swirl.
The sea forever sings, relentless and free,
A symphony woven with waves of the sea.

Chants from the Serene Expanse

In tranquil meadows where silence thrives,
Chants arise softly, the spirit revives.
Golden fields stretch, kissed by the sun,
Whispers of peace, in unison spun.

Mountains stand tall, guardians of time,
Echoes of wisdom in every chime.
Nature's own hymn, a sweet lullaby,
Carried on winds as they drift and sigh.

Clouds lazily roam in a vast azure dome,
Chants of the expanse invite us to roam.
Every heartbeat close, nature's embrace,
Time slows its march in this sacred place.

Stars scatter softly in twilight's glow,
Chants speak of wonders that few get to know.
The calm of the night, a celestial spun,
Cradling dreams and the tales left undone.

In this serene vastness, we find our light,
Chants from the expanse, guiding through night.
With every soft whisper, come let us hear,
The magic that lives in the moments so clear.

Kaleidoscope of Echoing Dreams

In twilight's embrace, colors collide,
A kaleidoscope of dreams where hopes reside.
Shadows and light dance in endless streams,
Crafting the fabric of echoing dreams.

Whispers of wishes float on the breeze,
Twinkling like stars, a cosmic tease.
Each moment a fragment, a vibrant thread,
Woven together in the things left unsaid.

The heart seeks the patterns, the shapes that inspire,
A colorful tapestry, weaving desire.
With every soft glance, the world shifts and sways,
Kaleidoscope visions ignite the bold ways.

Silent reflections on waters so deep,
Dreams softly murmur, inviting to leap.
While time gently folds, in layers it seems,
Creating a symphony of echoing dreams.

As night enfolds all in its velvety sway,
Each breath a reminder, a promise to play.
In the dance of the stars, find your own theme,
In the kaleidoscope of this whispering dream.

Harmony Under the Sky's Embrace

Beneath the branches wide and green,
We dance in shadows, soft and serene.
The whispers of leaves in the gentle breeze,
Carry our laughter, a symphony of ease.

Stars flicker above, a celestial guide,
In the embrace of night, where dreams reside.
We sway to the rhythm of the moon's soft glow,
Finding our peace in the ebb and flow.

Time slows to a hush, as we spin and twirl,
In this sacred space, our hearts start to unfurl.
Harmony blooms in the air we share,
Illuminated paths, in silence, we dare.

The sky holds secrets in its vast array,
Each glimmering light leads us on our way.
With every heartbeat, our spirits ignite,
Together we flourish in the stillness of night.

In unity's song, where all souls align,
We gather the moments, so precious, so fine.
In the arms of the stars, we find our true place,
In harmony's grasp, we embrace our grace.

Echoes of a Distant Horizon

Beyond the hills where the sun meets the sea,
Whispers of tales echo wild and free.
The waves speak volumes of journeys untold,
Drawing us near with their touch, soft yet bold.

Clouds drift like dreams, across the bright sky,
Beneath them we wander, you and I.
Each step leads us closer to shadows that dance,
Inviting our hearts into a daring romance.

The horizon beckons with colors so bright,
Painting the canvas of fading daylight.
In twilight's embrace, we leave fears behind,
As echoes of laughter and freedom unwind.

We chase after starlight, as night falls around,
In this realm of wonder, our spirits are found.
The universe hums, a melody sweet,
Where every heartbeat, a promise we meet.

With every sunrise, a new tale begins,
We carry the echoes, the joys, and the sins.
To the ends of the earth, we vow to remain,
Bound by the whispers, the love, and the pain.

Whispers in the Celestial Current

In the depth of night, where silence holds tight,
Whispers of stardust take flight in the light.
Galaxies twinkle, and dreams intertwine,
In the vastness above, your hand close to mine.

The cosmos spins gently, a timeless dance,
Every heartbeat echoes the chance for romance.
Caught in the current of celestial streams,
We ride the waves of our own midnight dreams.

Through the veil of the heavens, our spirits ascend,
In harmony flow, where beginnings won't end.
Infinite beauty, in each spark we find,
Binds us together, the hearts intertwined.

As whispers take shape in the quietest hush,
We breathe in the magic, in every soft rush.
The night sings our story, in cosmic refrain,
Carving our essence in memory's grain.

So let the stars cradle our hopes and our fears,
In this sacred moment, we shed all our tears.
For in the celestial current, we are entwined,
Whispers and echoes of love unconfined.

Songs of the Shimmering Veil

Through the shimmering veil, where the light softly plays,

We weave our stories in twilight's embrace.
Each note dances gently on the soft evening air,
A melody twines through the silence we share.

Stars start to shimmer, like gems in the night,
Guiding our whispers toward love's gentle light.
Hand in hand, we tread on the path of the stars,
Chasing the dreams that have taken us far.

In the glow of the moon, secrets come alive,
As we sing our songs, our souls revive.
A tapestry woven with laughter and sighs,
In the heart of the night, where our spirit flies.

The shimmering veil, a promise of more,
Opens the gateway to uncharted shores.
With each note we sing, our fears drift away,
In the warmth of the night, love lighting the way.

So let us be brave, let our voices unite,
In the songs of the shimmering veil, pure delight.
For in this sweet moment, together we stand,
Writing our story, heart in heart, hand in hand.

Enigmatic Chants of the Flowing Rivers

Whispers of water, secrets unfold,
Each ripple a story, each wave, a hold.
Beneath the moon's gaze, shadows waltz,
Echoes of ages, in silence they pulse.

Gentle currents dance, tracing the stones,
Carving their paths, like ancient tones.
Nature's soft hymn, in twilight's embrace,
Rivers remember, the past they trace.

In the twilight glow, reflections ignite,
Mirroring dreams in the soft, fading light.
Flowing like time, they journey on,
Echoing whispers till the break of dawn.

Secrets murmured in a soft, flowing stream,
Bearing the weight of a forgotten dream.
With every twist, with every turn,
The heart of the water, forever shall yearn.

Enigmas unravel where waters convene,
Binding the tales of the seen and unseen.
Ode to the currents, to ripples and tides,
In flowing rivers, the mystery abides.

Melodic Journeys Through the Ether

Notes in the breeze, melodies fly,
Whispering softly, beneath the wide sky.
Dancing with echoes, the spirit takes flight,
Carving a path through the dark of the night.

Stars hum a tune, harmonies collide,
Each shimmer a note, in the cosmic tide.
Interstellar songs in the vastness unfurl,
Carried on winds from another world.

Voices of stardust, the galaxies sing,
Rhythms of ages, of timeless spring.
In the depths of silence, the heart can hear,
The magic of music, drawing ever near.

Waves of vibrations, incidents blend,
Creating a canvas where journeys transcend.
Through the fabric of space, with passion they soar,
Melodic adventures forever explore.

Riding the currents, a soul full of dreams,
Drifting through eons, or so it seems.
In music we travel, through realms far and wide,
Ethereal pathways where spirit can glide.

Crescendos of Springs and Streams

Springtime awakens, life starts to hum,
Rivulets gurgle, as new flowers come.
Gentle vibrations in the fresh morning air,
Nature's crescendo, a symphony rare.

Butterflies flutter, birds sing on high,
Dancing through colors as moments fly by.
Springs bubbling forth, with laughter and grace,
Crafting a landscape in this sacred space.

Rippling waters weave through grasses and stones,
Melodies swirling in gentle undertones.
The heartbeat of spring, in every stream's flow,
Igniting the spirit with a soft, warm glow.

Crescendoing joys in the warm golden light,
In the arms of the earth, all wrongs are made right.
Nature's sweet ballad orchestrates cheer,
In springs and streams, all worries disappear.

Eagerly flowing, they gather and swirl,
A dance of enchantment, a water-born whirl.
Crescendos of life in every embrace,
A timeless reflection in nature's grace.

Tantalizing Vibes of Distant Shores

Waves crashing softly on golden sand beds,
Carrying whispers of faraway threads.
Tides full of secrets, caressing the coast,
Echoes of voyages, cherished the most.

Shells worn by time, where memories cling,
Each grain of sand, a tale to bring.
Breezes of salt, infused with the sun,
Tantalizing vibes where the sky meets the run.

Palms sway gently, a dance in the breeze,
Nature's own rhythm, a tranquil tease.
Laughter and music rise high in the air,
Inviting the heart to shed every care.

Distant horizons where dreams intertwine,
Footprints in sand, in a moment divine.
The ocean's embrace is both fierce and mild,
Tantalizing vibes that awaken the child.

Under the moonlight, the world feels alive,
The pulse of the sea, where spirits arrive.
With every wave's kiss, horizons explore,
In the dance of the tides, we always want more.

Odes to the Dancing Aquatic Veil

In twilight's grace, the waters sway,
A shimmering dance, in hues of gray.
With ripples bright, and whispers sweet,
The aquatic veil swirls in rhythmic beat.

Beneath the moon's soft silver gaze,
The waves perform in gentle praise.
Each droplet glimmers, a jeweled light,
A ballet of silk in the hush of night.

Waves weave stories, of joy and strife,
They conceal secrets, and echo life.
The fluid motion, a timeless lore,
A testament to what came before.

Embrace the current, let it steer,
In dancing waters, we conquer fear.
The aquatic veil calls, serene and bright,
Inviting the heart to take its flight.

So let us dive, with hearts full and free,
In this aquatic embrace, just you and me.
For in the depths, our spirits unite,
In the dance of waves, we find our light.

Anthems of the Liquid Harmony

A serenade sung by gentle streams,
The liquid whispers cradle our dreams.
In every ripple, a note, a chime,
Creating symphonies, transcending time.

The brooklet flows, a soft refrain,
Melody mingles with the falling rain.
In rhythms sweet, the waters play,
An anthem of peace in a world of gray.

With every splash, a heartbeat's song,
Inviting all souls to come along.
The harmony swells, a tide of grace,
Drawing the weary to this sacred place.

As sunlight dances on the liquid thread,
The anthems rise, a soothing spread.
Each wave a story, a note anew,
In the symphony of life, all hearts are true.

Together we flow, like rivers we blend,
In liquid harmony, we find our friends.
For in the depths, the music's embrace,
Guides us to find our rightful place.

Verses in the Shining Tides

Upon the shore where the waves collide,
Shimmering verses in the shining tides.
Each crest and trough, a line unfolds,
Tales of the sea, in whispers told.

The ocean's breath, a rhythmic hum,
Echoing secrets from whence we come.
The sands hold memories, shaped by time,
In the verses of tides, we find our rhyme.

Glowing shells, like words on a page,
Capture the magic of nature's stage.
The moonlit waters, a poet's delight,
In every wave, dreams take flight.

With every ebb, a heartbeat's call,
From the depths of the ocean, we rise and fall.
In the shimmering tides, we sing our song,
Of hope, of love, where we all belong.

So let us wander, hand in hand,
On the shores where shadows and light stand.
In verses shining, the ocean's lore,
Guides us forever to seek and explore.

Melodies Woven in Celestial Waters

In celestial streams where stardust flows,
Melodies awaken as twilight glows.
The water sings with a vibrant hue,
Crafting an opus, both old and new.

Each droplet carries a tale profound,
Of ancient worlds, where dreams abound.
The currents whisper, a soft embrace,
In the dance of water, our souls find space.

With every wave, a heart's desire,
Stirred by the cosmos, igniting fire.
The melodies weave, like threads of gold,
In celestial waters, the stories unfold.

The stars above twinkle in time,
As waves harmonize in festive rhyme.
Together we drift, as one we flow,
In the melodies woven, our spirits grow.

So let us merge with this cosmic stream,
Where every note enhances the dream.
In celestial waters, forever we'll sway,
In woven melodies, we'll find our way.

Ballads of the Glorious Cascade

Amidst the mountain's rise, a song does flow,
Whispers of water, where soft breezes blow.
Each droplet dances, a shimmering chase,
In nature's embrace, a time-stopping grace.

Legends unfold with each thunderous crash,
Echoing beauty in bubbles that splash.
The spirit of earth sings through valleys wide,
As the cascade's heart beats, it will not hide.

Sunlight ignites a cascade of dreams,
Painting the world with its golden beams.
Life thrives around, in each corner and curve,
A ballad of water, the essence we serve.

The call of the wild, a siren's delight,
Canyons and cliffs join in the glorious sight.
Nature's orchestra plays, a symphonic flow,
With every soft splash, the wonder will grow.

Forever entwined in the ages of time,
The Glorious Cascade, a story in rhyme.
In heartbeats of rivers, we find our place,
In every soft sigh, there's magic and grace.

Echoes in the Prism of Twilight

When daylight wanes and shadows creep,
Whispers of secrets begin to peep.
Stars twinkle gently, a soft serenade,
In the twilight's embrace, all worries fade.

Colors merge softly, horizon aglow,
A canvas of dreams in the evening's flow.
The moon rises high, casting silver light,
Echoes of nightfall, a dance of delight.

Through whispers of breezes, the stories weave,
Painting the sky, they entice and deceive.
In the prism of twilight, a world anew,
Magic awakens, as darkness breaks through.

Time stands suspended, as worlds unfold,
A tapestry woven with threads of gold.
Laughter of crickets and rustling leaves,
In twilight's soft arms, the heart quietly believes.

As night settles in with its soothing grace,
The echoes of twilight take their place.
Mirrored reflections on the still pond's face,
In the calm of the evening, we find our space.

Orchestrations Along the Gleaming Edge

Upon the horizon, where earth meets the sky,
A symphony whispers as clouds drift by.
Melodies mingle with the sunlight's gold,
Orchestrations thrive in the brave and the bold.

Each breeze carries notes of a distant song,
Harmonies shimmer, inviting us along.
Strumming the strands of the twilight's loom,
Crafting a world from the whispering bloom.

With every step taken, the chorus resounds,
Nature composing its symphony's bounds.
Voices of mountains, of rivers, and trees,
Dance to the rhythm, embraced by the breeze.

Underneath the stars, where silence prevails,
The heartbeats of shadows etch glorious trails.
Orchestrated magic in the night's sweet embrace,
Echoes of dreams in this radiant space.

As dawn approaches, the music transforms,
With colors and light, in new shapes it warms.
The gleaming edge glows, a promise of morn,
Orchestrations eternal, anew every dawn.

Rhythms of the Clearwater Vale

In the heart of the vale, where the waters flow,
Rhythms emerge in the quiet glow.
Songs of the streams murmur sweet and clear,
A symphony rising, for all who draw near.

Rolling hills cradle the soft, gentle breeze,
Echoes of laughter in rustling leaves.
Each ripple and wave joins the joyful song,
In rhythms of life, where we all belong.

Sunlight cascades on the surface so bright,
Painting the vale in vibrant delight.
The heart of the earth beats in sync with the light,
A dance of creation, both sacred and bright.

Through shadows of trees, the melodies thrive,
In Clearwater Vale, all spirits come alive.
Carried by currents that sway and entwine,
The rhythms of nature, forever divine.

As day turns to dusk, the echoes remain,
In the stillness of night, they call out again.
Rhythms of the vale, a soft lullaby,
In dreams they will linger, 'neath the vast sky.

A Symphony in the Morning Dew

Whispers of dawn, so sweet and clear,
Gentle breezes, nature's cheer.
Each droplet glimmers, a tiny pearl,
Awakening dreams as the day unfurls.

Birds sing softly, a symphonic rise,
Painting the heavens with melodic sighs.
Sunlight dances on petals bright,
Awakening colors, a joyous sight.

The world breathes softly, so pure, so new,
Wrapped in warmth of morning's hue.
A tapestry woven, each thread a song,
A symphony in dew, where all belong.

The earth stirs gently, a yawn, a stretch,
Nature's embrace, a heartfelt sketch.
With each heartbeat, life starts to flow,
A symphony born in the morning glow.

In stillness, wonder, we find our way,
Guided by light of the breaking day.
Each moment cherished, a gift from above,
In the morning dew, we find our love.

Serene Whirlwinds of Memory

In quiet corners of the mind,
Serene whispers are intertwined.
Moments captured, faint and bright,
Swirling gently, like shadows of light.

Familiar faces drift like dust,
In the embrace of soft, sweet trust.
Laughter echoes in quiet refrain,
Carried softly on the gentle rain.

Through winding paths of time we roam,
In these whirlwinds, we find our home.
Every heartbeat a story untold,
In the tapestry, memories unfold.

A dance of time, so bittersweet,
Where joy and sorrow meet.
We cherish the moments, both lost and found,
In serene whirlwinds, love is bound.

Nostalgia wraps us in a warm embrace,
A tender touch, a fleeting grace.
In every whisper, we find the thread,
Sewn in the fabric of words unsaid.

Floating Notes of an Endless Sky

Winds carry whispers from afar,
Melodies birthed among the stars.
Floating notes on a canvas blue,
Dreams and wishes, a soft debut.

Clouds become instruments, gentle and sweet,
Strumming the sky with a rhythmic beat.
Each breeze a song, each gust a sigh,
An endless concert beneath the sky.

Harmony flows like a river wide,
Tides of time in a blissful ride.
With every flutter, a story blooms,
In the silence, the heart resumes.

Stars twinkle softly, in the night's embrace,
Echoes of music, a fleeting trace.
Floating notes like dreams in flight,
Under the canvas of starry night.

In every moment lies a refrain,
A dance of joy, a touch of pain.
Beneath the heavens, we find our way,
In floating notes, forever we sway.

Glistening Harmonies at Dusk

As shadows lengthen and day departs,
Glistening harmonies fill our hearts.
The sun sinks slowly, a fiery blaze,
Painting the sky in a golden haze.

Whispers of twilight, soft and low,
Nature hums as the stars start to glow.
Crickets chirp, a sweet lullaby,
In the quiet moments, time slips by.

Colors merge in a dazzling display,
As night embraces the closing day.
Every breath a note, every sigh a song,
In this twilight, we all belong.

The world glistens in soft twilight's hue,
In the dance of dusk, we find what's true.
A symphony wrapped in subtle grace,
In glistening harmonies, we find our place.

As the stars twinkle like gemstones rare,
We gather dreams in the cool night air.
With hearts wide open, we claim the dusk,
In the glistening harmonies, love's gentle husk.

Resonance of the Luminous Depths

In the blue abyss, whispers gleam,
Echoes of light that softly beam.
Stars buried deep in the ocean's chest,
Calling the lost to find their rest.

Rippling currents weave their song,
A symphony where shadows belong.
Fragments of fate dance through the night,
Guiding the weary with gentle light.

Tides ebb and flow, a breath of grace,
As moonlight's fingers trace each face.
In depths uncharted, hope still glows,
A promise kept where the current flows.

Silent guardians of stories untold,
Secrets of ages shimmering bold.
In the embrace of the sea's cool breath,
We find our truths in the whisper of death.

In luminous depths where wonders play,
Our hearts resonate in a vibrant sway.
With every wave that kisses the shore,
We listen closely, we hear more.

Odes to the Ethereal Glimmer

Glistening jewels in the dawn's first light,
Scattering dreams, taking flight.
Each beam a tale waiting to unfold,
In shadows of silver, whispers of gold.

Waking to shimmer, the world becomes bright,
Painting our paths with strokes of pure white.
Under the gaze of the morning sun,
Ethereal glimmers have just begun.

Uplifted spirits in radiant dance,
Every moment holds a delicate chance.
In the silence, beauty refrains,
An echo of love through the gentle rains.

Float through the cosmos, embrace the divine,
With stars as guides, our hearts intertwine.
In an endless sea of twinkling light,
We weave our dreams, our hopes ignite.

As sunset weaves colors in the sky,
We gather memories, letting them fly.
With odes to the glimmer, we're never alone,
In twilight's embrace, we find our home.

Tranquil Voices from the Water's Surface

Rippling reflections in still, clear pools,
Nature's secrets wrapped in gentle rules.
Beneath the shimmer, whispers reside,
Where serenity lives, and dreams abide.

Graceful swirls in the evening's calm,
Each voice a note, a silent balm.
Ripples of laughter, soft as a sigh,
Unfolding tales as the moments fly.

Birds take flight from the edge of the shore,
While silence speaks of what came before.
Leaves dance slowly in the cool, sweet air,
Tranquil voices drift with a knowing care.

Every glance casts a story anew,
In pools of reflection, life flows through.
As twilight falls, shadows take form,
In the arms of stillness, we are reborn.

Listen closely to water's deep song,
Echoes of wisdom where we all belong.
In tranquil moments, our spirits find peace,
In the heart of the stillness, we find release.

Cadence in the Softest Shadows

In twilight's embrace, the world holds its breath,
Soft whispers linger, a dance with death.
Shadows entwined with the night's gentle sigh,
Echoes of secrets beneath the vast sky.

Each moment a cadence, a heartbeat so sweet,
As darkness weaves magic around our feet.
Ebbing and flowing, the rhythm of dreams,
In the solace of night, everything gleams.

Flickers of hope dance in quiet reserve,
Beneath the soft veil, our passions curve.
In shadowed corners where wonders reside,
We find our truth with the stars as our guide.

The moon softly hums to the slumbering trees,
Cradling the dreams on a gentle breeze.
In the softest shadows, the heart starts to sing,
Celebrating life in the joys that we bring.

As dawn peeks through with a burst of light,
We awake to the whispers that end the night.
With cadence in shadows, our spirits are free,
In the dance of the world, we find harmony.

Soliloquies of the Evening Songbirds

In the hush of dusk, they sing,
Whispers of the day's soft end.
Notes like petals on the breeze,
Carried where the shadows blend.

With each flutter, tales unfold,
Of love, of loss, of dreams once told.
A chorus swells, the night ignites,
In melodies of golden light.

Through leafy boughs, their voices play,
A serenade to end the day.
Echoes dance in the cooling air,
As twilight lingers, soft and rare.

From branch to branch, they take their flight,
In colors bold against the night.
Filling hearts with gentle ease,
Their songs are woven through the trees.

A symphony of peace and grace,
In every note, a warm embrace.
The evening blooms, a tender sight,
As songbirds sing their soft goodnight.

Glistening Lullabies of the Twilight Hour

Dusk wraps the earth in silken threads,
Stars peek out, their secrets spread.
A lullaby begins to weave,
Through heart and mind, the night's reprieve.

Moonlight drips like honey sweet,
Kissing the ground with gentle feet.
With every note, the world sighs low,
As dreams awaken, soft and slow.

Crickets join in rhythmic hum,
A serenade for night to come.
Their music drifts through the dense air,
Binding souls with tender care.

Restful whispers ride the breeze,
Carrying hopes, like autumn leaves.
In this twilight, peace finds home,
In glistening lullabies we roam.

Every star a wish fulfilled,
The heart enchanted, softly thrilled.
Wrapped in shadows, love's embrace,
In twilight's arms, we find our place.

Astral Harmonies in Hidden Valleys

Deep in valleys, where shadows play,
Celestial songs light the way.
Stars ignite the darkened skies,
Crafting dreams that softly rise.

Whispers float on gentle streams,
Carrying the night's sweet dreams.
Each note a journey, tales untold,
In harmony, the night unfolds.

Mountains echo with cosmic sound,
In the quiet, life's joys abound.
A symphony of stars and trees,
Where hearts can rest and spirits ease.

The moonlight bathes the world in glow,
Caressing souls that drift and flow.
In hidden valleys, peace is found,
As nightingale sings, profound.

Through astral paths, we wander free,
Embraced in nature's melody.
In hidden realms, beneath the skies,
Harmonies of night arise.

Ballads of the Everlasting Gale

Whispers of the wind, a tune,
Crafted softly beneath the moon.
Wandering through fields of gold,
The stories of the earth retold.

Breath of ages, wild and wide,
In every gust, the tales reside.
A ballad sings of time and space,
Journeying forth to find its place.

Through mountains high and valleys low,
The everlasting gale will flow.
A symphony through trees so grand,
In harmony with nature's hand.

From oceans deep to skies above,
The wind carries whispers of love.
In every corner of the land,
The ballads echo, soft and grand.

A melody born of earth and sky,
In the gentle breeze, we learn to fly.
An endless song, forever near,
In every gust, the truth we hear.

Illuminated Echoes in the Mist

Through the fog, soft whispers call,
Shadows dance, where memories fall.
Glimmers of light, a fleeting sight,
In stillness, dreams take flight.

From the depths, they rise and gleam,
A tapestry woven, a tangled dream.
Echoes linger in the chill,
Painting silence with a thrill.

Nature's breath, a canvas bare,
Each moment caught, a heart laid bare.
In tranquil hues, emotions blend,
Within this mist, dark paths amend.

Dances of Light on Liquid Canvas

In ripples small, reflections sway,
Colors twirl in a bright ballet.
Each shimmer dips, then springing fast,
A union formed, a bond that's cast.

Liquid gold beneath the sun,
In liquid dreams, we are all one.
Brush strokes wild, the water sings,
As stars join in this dance of things.

Gentle waves whisper secrets fair,
While hearts unite with every glare.
A symphony in motion flows,
As painted light forever glows.

Harmonies Flowing Through the Air

Soft notes weave through gentle breeze,
A melody that puts hearts at ease.
With every breath, a song takes flight,
Painting echoes in the night.

The world hums in a sweet refrain,
Linking souls in joy and pain.
Invisible threads of sound entwine,
Creating moments, pure and divine.

Notes collide in vibrant arcs,
Filling silence with gentle sparks.
Harmony calls, we heed its plea,
In the dance of life, set free.

Melodic Ripples of Time

In the pond of days gone by,
Ripples echo, soft and shy.
Moments captured, fleeting grace,
In waters deep, we find our place.

Each circle spreads, a tale to tell,
As memories rise from where they dwell.
Time's gentle hand, it shapes the flow,
In waves of past, our spirits glow.

With every splash, a heartbeat sounds,
In reflective pools, our joy abounds.
Melodic whispers through shadows churn,
As the tides of time forever turn.

Chants from the Glinting Abyss

Whispers dance in shadowed light,
Echoes sing of endless night.
Depths conceal a muted song,
Where the lost and dreamers long.

Waves caress the darkened stone,
Guarding secrets, all alone.
Currents weave their mystic thread,
Binding tales of love and dread.

Ghostly forms glide through the mist,
Yearning hearts that can't resist.
Voices fade, yet still they call,
In the void, we rise and fall.

Stars align with silent grace,
Bearing witness to our face.
In the chasms of the sea,
Hopes are woven, wild and free.

Through the dark, the glinting sings,
Of the joy that sorrow brings.
Beneath the depths, in quiet air,
Chants of longing lay bare.

Nocturnes of the Serene Deep

Beneath the waves, the moonlight glows,
Softly where the night wind blows.
Gentle lapping on the shore,
Sings of peace forevermore.

In the stillness, dreams take flight,
Cradled in the arms of night.
Serenity, a tender balm,
Whispers sweetly, holds us calm.

Stars peek through the velvet dark,
Filling hearts with gentle spark.
In this realm, the spirit flies,
Painting hopes across the skies.

Lullabies of shadowed waves,
Rock us softly, soothe like graves.
Here we linger, fears allayed,
In the hush, our souls displayed.

Every drop a tale unfolds,
In the deep, a truth that holds.
Nocturnes blend in perfect flow,
As the tides of silence grow.

Harmonies of the Glistening Shore

Windswept grasses sway and bend,
To the rhythm, hearts ascend.
Footprints tracing in the sand,
Songs of nature, free and grand.

Crystal waves embrace the night,
Dancing under starlit light.
Each crest carries dreams anew,
Harmonies of me and you.

Morning rays on water play,
Chasing shadows, night gives way.
Seagulls call, a symphony,
Echoing eternity.

Every shell holds whispered tales,
Of the sea and gentle gales.
In their depths, true stories blend,
Bringing solace, love, and mend.

Harmonies of shorelines blaze,
Crafting moments, sunlit days.
As the tide ebbs and it flows,
In our hearts, the magic grows.

Songs from the Silvered Depths

In the hush of liquid dreams,
Mysteries stitch vibrant seams.
Silver currents, whispers low,
Guide us where the deep tides flow.

Glimmers spark in depths unseen,
Every moment, soft and keen.
Songs of ancient mariners,
Echo in the ocean's stir.

Diving deep into the blue,
Searching for a truth so true.
Silver shadows, glimmering bright,
Dancing softly in the night.

Fragments of a world unknown,
Calls from depths that feel like home.
Every note a part of lore,
In the waves, we search for more.

Voices rise from ocean's breath,
Carrying both life and death.
Songs from depths that drown our fears,
Orca's calls, the sound of years.

Lullabies of the Hidden Depths

In the quiet depths of night,
Whispers weave a gentle light,
Stars are cloaked in velvet dreams,
Flowing softly like the streams.

Sleep now, child, drift away,
The moon guards you, night and day,
Underneath the silver skies,
Hushed are all your softest cries.

Secrets held by ocean's breath,
Sung by shadows, life, and death,
Waves will cradle you in peace,
Let the world around you cease.

Echoes trembling on the shore,
Calling gently evermore,
Feel the treasure in the dark,
Hope and wonder, every spark.

Lullabies in soft embrace,
Guide you to a tranquil place,
In the depths where dreams abide,
Find the comfort locked inside.

Reverberations Among the Stars

In the silence of the night,
Stars awaken, shining bright,
Whispers travel on the breeze,
Carried far across the seas.

Cosmic dances draw us near,
Voices echo, crystal clear,
Galaxies spin tales untold,
In their shimmer, dreams unfold.

Radiance in endless gloom,
Hope and wonder gently loom,
Celestial paths intertwine,
Guiding hearts with hands divine.

Every star, a story born,
In the dark, new life is worn,
Reverberations sing in waves,
Of the journeys that each craves.

Feel the pulse of worlds afar,
As we reach for every star,
United in this grand expanse,
We entwine in cosmic dance.

Caresses of the Gentle Breeze

Softly whispers through the trees,
Dancing lightly, gentle breeze,
Carrying the scent of bloom,
Filling hearts with life's perfume.

Touch of warmth upon the skin,
Breath of nature drawing in,
Every sigh, a sweet embrace,
In the stillness, find your place.

Leaves are rustling, secrets shared,
In the quiet, hearts are bared,
Nature's song, a lullaby,
Beneath the vast and open sky.

Feel the currents as they flow,
Guiding dreams where shadows go,
In the dance of dusk's retreat,
Find the rhythm, pulse, and beat.

Caresses pure, like whispered prayer,
Embrace the breeze with tender care,
Let it lift you, set you free,
In its depth, find harmony.

Ephemeral Chimes of the Evening

As daylight fades to twilight's grace,
Soft chimes echo in their place,
Moments fleeting, time to weave,
In the dusk, we learn to believe.

Whispers carried on the night,
Glimmers of a fading light,
Stars like chimes in sky's embrace,
Resonate in dreamlike space.

Open hearts receive the song,
Where the fleeting notes belong,
Every moment, sweet and rare,
Ephemeral, suspended air.

Time will dance and then depart,
Leaving echoes in the heart,
Chimes of evening, soft and sweet,
Mark the moments, feel the beat.

In the twilight, memories blend,
Sending whispers with the wind,
This evening's song, a tender friend,
In its magic, find the end.

Starry Cadence in the Night

Beneath the velvet sky we gaze,
Stars twinkle like whispers in a maze.
The moon dances softly on shadows cast,
Time holds its breath, moments amassed.

Dreams take flight on the night's cool breeze,
Carried away to mysterious seas.
Each twinkling light tells a tale untold,
Of wishes made and hearts bold.

Crickets sing tunes in rhythmic delight,
As darkness unfolds with a shimmery light.
Night wraps around like a gentle embrace,
While we lose ourselves in this vast space.

Constellations play in the cosmic dance,
Guiding our hearts in a tender romance.
Each star a note in the night's sweet song,
In this cadence of calm, we belong.

In the silence, our spirits ignite,
With the stars overhead, our dreams take flight.
As dawn approaches, the magic will fade,
But the echoes of night in our hearts are laid.

Fluid Verses in the Twilight

The horizon melts in hues of gold,
Whispers of twilight, stories unfold.
Shadows lengthen and colors blend,
In this fleeting moment, time suspends.

Thoughts like rivers drift and sway,
As day gently bows to night's ballet.
Every heartbeat echoes the day's refrain,
In this twilight, there's beauty in pain.

The stars awaken, one by one,
Their soft glow hints at the night's fun.
We share our dreams in a twilight hush,
In the stillness, our hearts softly rush.

With every breath, the air feels light,
In fluid verses, we take flight.
As the world around begins to rest,
We find solace in this gentle quest.

Moments linger, like stories told,
In the twilight's embrace, we are bold.
Holding hands, we leave, yet we stay,
In fluid verses that never decay.

Undercurrents of Dream and Desire

In the depths of night, secrets glide,
Undercurrents swirl, where dreams reside.
Whispers of wishes entwine and dance,
Drawing us closer in this trance.

Desire flickers like a candle's flame,
Igniting our hearts, urging us to claim.
Moments suspended, time flows anew,
In these currents, I find my way to you.

The ocean of dreams pulls us near,
With every wave, I can feel you here.
The rhythm of hearts beats soft and true,
In this sanctuary, it's just us two.

Chasing the shadows that flicker and fade,
In the night's embrace, our fears are laid.
With each heartbeat, the world fades away,
As undulating tides lead us astray.

So let us drift on this sea of desire,
Navigating the depths, lifting higher.
Together we'll sail 'neath the starlit sky,
In the current of dreams, you and I.

Tides of Time Whispering Softly

In the hush of the dusk, time flows slow,
Tides whisper secrets only we know.
Ebbing and flowing with memories clear,
Each moment a ripple, my dear.

The sands of time slip through our hands,
Holding the moments like fragile strands.
We gather the twilight, savor the peace,
As time's gentle currents grant us release.

With every heartbeat, time will unfold,
Stories of laughter, of love, and of gold.
Softly they linger, these whispers divine,
In the tides of time, your heart is entwined.

Let waves carry us to places unknown,
In the sea of our dreams, we've beautifully grown.
With the moon as our witness, we stand side by side,
In the tides of time, let's take this ride.

So hear the whispers of the hours past,
In the tides of time, let our love last.
As stars blink above, in a symphony bright,
We dance with the tides in the velvet night.

www.ingramcontent.com/pod-product-compliance
Ingram Content Group UK Ltd.
Pitfield, Milton Keynes, MK11 3LW, UK
UKHW021536210125
4208UKWH00025B/673

9 781805 596776